MW01132879

BECOME

THE

LIAISON

OF CHOICE

ROSALIND STOKES

Also by Rosalind Stokes

Structuring Your Gospel Mime Ministry

The Short & Sweet of Gospel Mime

To Jace and Ayven:

I am excited to have the opportunity to impact your lives on purpose. And I am overjoyed about the Loving men that I know you will grow up to be.

I Love You,

Grandma

ACKNOWLEDGEMENTS

Writing this book would not have been possible without the amazing God that I serve. My appreciation to my supervisors, I couldn't have been successful without you being supportive and encouraging. Thank you for believing in me and for your insight and guidance over the years. Thank you to my family and friends that allowed me to be true to self. Thank you for your love and unwavering support.

CONTENTS

<u>List 200 Things that you want</u>

_____

_____

_____

_____

_____

_____

_____

_____

_____

_____

_____

_____

_____

What are you willing to go through to get the things on your list?

Notes:_____

My Message to you

The Liaison position will look much different in the next 3-5 years. Hospitals and Skilled Nursing Facility's (SNF) will develop preferred provider relationships so facilities won't need as many liaisons as they do now. These facilities will want the best liaisons available (The Liaison of Choice) to manage the high volume of referrals.

The SNF's that don't have the preferred provider connection will really need to have that amazing Liaison of Choice. This Liaison must be able to add crucial value to the company. They must be critical thinkers. They would have to be able to secure patients in the hospitals that have preferred providers. We show you how to do just that by partnering with the preferred facilities and capturing the market in the community before they get to the hospital. Your patients will call you on the way to the hospital and they will let the hospital know that they want to be referred to your services.

If you want to be a liaison in this upcoming age you will need to make that quantum leap now. You must set yourself apart from the rest.

What is the #1 Cause of Stress in Your Life?

Choices!!

Think about what has caused you stress in the last 30 days. It can either be traced back to a choice that you made or it will go back to how you chose to react to a situation.

Example: You or someone you love has been diagnosed with a life threatening illness.

You could choose to:

Fight it and get involved in raising money to find a cure.

OR

Roll up in a ball and die.

When you find that you have made the wrong choice, you can always change it.

That would be your choice.

Why Have A LIAISON?

What is the purpose of a Liaison?

The Liaison is entrusted with two of the most crucial parts of the business:

1. Patient reimbursement rate.

2. Types of patients.

They find new business opportunities for the organization.

This critical thinking Liaison is responsible for two things.

    1. Capturing the right patient at the right time.

    2. Sending patients to the right location.

What will the Liaison Position Look Like in 5 Years?

Hospitals and Rehabilitation Centers will develop cost sharing modules in an effort to decrease the cost of medical care and the stress of patients returning to the hospital unnecessarily. The facilities of choice will be those that have a proven track record of excellent care and a low return rate to the hospital.

TIMELINESS

You are the initial decision maker.

You should be able to give the referral source an answer based on your initial assessment without going through someone else. Use your facility Clinical Capability Sheet.

Clinical Capability Sheet

Facility: Beverly Hills Nursing Center:

Skill:	Green	Yellow	Red
Ventilator Management	x		
Automatic External Defibrillator			x
Alcohol/Substance Abuse		x	
Bariatric Care	x		
Bi-Pap/CPAP	x		
Bladder Irrigation		x	
Closed Head Injury		x	
Gastrostomy Tube	x		
Hemodialysis In-house	x		

Green - You can say yes.

Yellow - You need to consult with the facility.

Red - Can not care for the patient (Know what facilities that can care for this patient and give that information to the referral source).

In most cases, you should be answering the referral source within 15 minutes

Other time tables should be established at your facilities. What are they?

- Insurance approval
- Medication acceptance
- Respiratory, DON, HD, or other discipline approvals
- Expected date of transfer
- Room / bed assigned report to nurse
- Etc.

KNOW YOUR STUFF

Know your Competitors and your Facilities

Tour and gather the statistics on every SNF (Skilled Nursing Facility) within at least a 25 mile radius of your locations.

Use this data to create your business development strategy. You will be selling your Benefits vs Features against these centers regularly. **It just makes sense that you know what they offer and how you differ, right?**

There will come a time when you don't have what the customer needs or wants.

You have a choice to:

1. Convince the customer that they are better off with your services.
2. You don't let the customer know that your competitor has what they are looking for.

OR Chose To:

3. Gracefully provide them with your competitors name, number and contact persons information. Let them know if things don't work out they should feel free to call you. Obtain permission to reach out to them in the next 72 hours to check on them. Call the competitor to make them aware of the referral.

   Note what the service is that your facility couldn't provide and be sure to inform the facility decision makers. Analyze as to whether or not you should be developing a program to meet the need.

   The 3rd choice could result in you losing the admission but gain the respect and trust of the customer and your referral source.

Develop Partnerships

Partner with any Assisted Living Facility (ALF), Long-Term Care Acute Center (LTAC) units, senior buildings-organizations, dialysis centers, hospice companies, methadone clinics, homeless shelters, doctors offices and other nursing facilities that you can build a relationship with. What companies have your facilities been referring patients to once they are ready to discharge from your SNF?

These companies should be referring to you as well.

New Employees

Meet your team:

Exchange cell numbers with the: Executive Director, Business Office Manager, Medicaid Specialist, Admission Director, Director of Nursing (DON), Social Worker, Back up Team, Administrator in training, Educator and Liaisons.

Know and get a copy of their Clinical Skills and the Guardian Angel Room Assignments (The department heads are assigned to make customer service rounds daily on assigned rooms).

Essential to Start your Liaison Position:

1. What was the market share prior to you starting? Use this information to gauge your Business Development Plan to exceed these numbers.

2. Ahd.com /Via Direct analytics on your hospital accounts - develop your market share strategy for your accounts. Be sure that your goals are measurable. This report provides critical information to assist you in your account management. It tells you: Number of beds, what categories of care they provide, number of employees (this is how many sales opportunities you have in 1 account), total discharges, total patients days, C-Suite employees, the affiliates, number and types of payers admitted, top 3 zip codes of their patients (market to this zip code so the patient knows about you before admitting into the hospital). Dissect the report to see what you can find that will assist you in

marketing to this account vertically and externally.

Ahd.com /Via Direct Analytics

Use this report to make your marketing strategy for your hospitals and the community.

This is the strongest defense in capturing the market share once hospitals create their preferred provider relationships.

You will market to the zip codes of the patients that go to that particular hospital. Contact churches, clubs, senior programs, colleges, recreation centers, host an art show for schools of all ages, etc.

Example: Goggle senior organizations within a 25 mile radius of 20032 zip code.

Inpatient Origin for Top 3 Zip Codes
Medicare Hospital Market Service Area File for calendar year ending 12/31/2018 / Definitions

ZIP Code of Residence	Discharges	Days of Care	Charges	Discharges Inc/(Dec)	Market Share
20032	577	3,772	$19,882,135	-7.7%	25.1%
20020	502	2,966	$16,406,571	-7.7%	17.2%
20019	203	1,600	$7,736,188	2.0%	5.9%

Outpatient Utilization Statistics by APC

Print them off and work your way through your list.

Get your contact names and numbers and start making appointments.
Analyze the report and identify the Who-What-When-Where and Why.
Who - target the diagnosis's that generate the highest reimbursement rate to your facility.

What service does the hospital need?

And **Why**?

When should the service be offered?

Where is my target customer located?

Complete your pre-call plan and you're on your way.

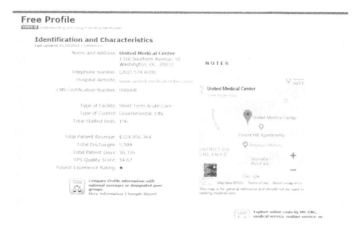

Joint Commission Accreditation
Accreditation status licensed from The Joint Commission
Last updated 10/08/2019 / Definitions and Terms of Use
  • Current Status: 09/23/2017 - Accreditation with Full Standards Compliance

Verified Trauma Program
Definitions
  • No data are available

Use coding indicators and
comparative data to identify areas
for improvement
More Information | Sample Report

Inpatient Utilization Statistics by Medical Service
Definitions

	Number Medicare Inpatients	Average Length of Stay	Average Charges	Medicare Case Mix Index (CMI)
Cardiology	384	4.85	$23,707	1.3464
Medicine	554	6.47	$35,329	1.6503
Neurology	94	5.99	$28,917	1.2434
Oncology	12	11.83	$46,228	1.8110
Orthopedic Surgery	19	9.00	$63,661	2.8455
Orthopedics	31	4.35	$21,514	1.1182
Psychiatry	217	8.23	$17,185	1.1403
Pulmonology	207	5.78	$31,318	1.5277
Surgery	87	12.86	$96,972	5.6735
Urology	129	6.47	$26,288	1.2667
Vascular Surgery	39	7.82	$55,339	3.0275
Total	1,784	6.60	$32,976	1.7042

Beds and Patient Days by Unit
Definitions

	Available Beds	Inpatient Days
HOSPITAL (including swing beds)		
Routine Services	180	26,990
Special Care	16	3,336
Nursery		0
Total Hospital	196	30,326

Financial Statistics
Definitions

	$	%
Gross Patient Revenue	$324,956,364	87.6
Non-Patient Revenue	$46,185,956	12.4
Total Revenue	$371,142,320	
Net Income (or Loss)	$-10,896,861	-2.9

This hospital is closing

$10,896,861 in the red

3. Pull the Medicare.gov.com report on your facilities and your competitors.

4. Tour your facilities and your competitors.

5. Your name tag is worn on the right upper chest. Make it easy on others, some people have trouble remembering names. When you are shaking their hand, their eyes can go right to your name tag. It also provides a continuity of care in reporting. When all employees wear their name tags in the same location, the customer has a clear location to identify who you are.

Maintaining Your Resources

1. Resource binder-onboard sheets, admission log, referral log, insurance reference sheet with what it covers and the reimbursement rate, high cost medication list, check list for parental infusion, dialysis and ventilator centers and Guardian Angel Assignments.

2. Business Cards, Cell phone and brochures.

3. The previous 2 years market share reports.

4. Your Job Description

5. New hires have approximately 40-60 days to prove themselves. Stay Organized.

NOTE: If you are new to a company gather as much of this information prior to starting as you can. Many companies start you in the field sooner than you expect. (**The Sink or Swim Method of Training**).

Let's Get Prepared

Smile while you are setting up your voice mail "Hello, thank you for choosing_____ you have reached _____Say Name & Title. If this is an emergency, please hang up and call 911. If this is not an emergency, please leave your name and a message so I can return your call as quickly as possible. Thank you for choosing "Your Company Name."

Not "I will call you at my convenience."

What does that say to the customer?

Dress for Success

No Gum – If your mouth gets dry use mints.

No Cleavage – no short skirts or dresses (refer to your company policy on the dress code).

NO Tight/baggy/wrinkled clothing-gaps between buttons.

Dress on the level of the customer or 1 above.

Look at yourself before you leave the house.

If there is any question as to whether you are dressed for success or not take it off.

No expensive Jewelry **unless** it's a wedding ring.

What could happen if you dress too far above a case manager?

The Director Of Nursing Meeting

Exchange numbers.

Verify the Clinical Skills Sheet

Ask: What are some positive/negative experiences that you have had with other liaisons?

What is the Director Of Nursing expecting from you?

Share your onboarding process.

Be sure that you communicate that you are part of the team and that you will refer patients that their staff can care for.

This is the perfect opportunity to be sure that both of you are on the same page. This meeting will lay the ground work towards your new relationship.

The Director of Nursing (DON) MUST feel comfortable with you sending patients. You will get pushback on referrals when they don't.

The Executive Director Admissions Director Meeting

These are your Operational thinking Leaders.

Exchange Numbers.

Share your onboard process with them and be sure they are aware that you use your critical thinking skills to determine what referrals to send to their facility. They should know that you are trained to assess patients clinically, financially and socially. Review the previous market share data and present your business development plan. Remember to obtain the dates and times of the facility Business Development Meetings so you can attend them.

The Critical Thinking Liaison doesn't
shoot from the hip.
We are Sharpe Shooters!

We are not Gun fighters, we are Inde-
pendent Business owners that companies place a great deal of **TRUST** in.
We manage the financial front end of
their business.
**Run your position like a responsible
business owner!**

Best Practice In Communication

Your Speech

You need more than talent and effort to make it to the next level. You must learn to speak differently to open the doors of opportunity. Your willingness to do this could mean the difference between success and failure. The way that you communicate can sabotage the most talented liaison and accelerate an average one. So let's begin with the end in mind. Everything that you do as a liaison is on purpose including the way that you connect with others through speech. Ask yourself, how is it that someone with less talent then you is further along than you? As you develop as a liaison, you are creating your brand. Your speech/voice is how you speak to yourself and the world around you. Your voice in fact is your brand. Successful liaisons speak differently and because they do, opportunities present themselves to them more easily. If you could get in a time machine and go back to speak to your younger self what advice would you give? OK, since the time machine hasn't been invented yet, how about you speak to your younger liaison self. What would you say? Would you be sure to stress the idea that our choices are the number one cause of stress in our jobs? If so, let them know that they can always change their choices when they find that they have turned left instead of right. Or, maybe you would stress the fact that now you know how important it is to master the skill of communication.

You are more than capable.

Studies show that women tend to underestimate their own potential as opposed to men. If you think that you are better than you are then you will rise to the occasion. You will communicate with more confidence and others will believe that you are more capable too. This will lead to more doors opening for you. Stop underestimating yourself. The most successful liaisons know what they bring to the table and what skills they still need to acquire. The fact that you are reading this book tells me that you are positioning yourself to be one of the top liaisons. Your internal beliefs about yourself will influence your external success.

I have worked with many Admissions Directors over the years. There was one in particular that I truly enjoyed working with because she knew her stuff. It was easy to get patients in her building and she knew her job inside and out. A year after I started with the company Stella went out on maternity leave with her second child. Once she returned to work, I saw how much time she spent at work instead of her spending time with her newborn and her family. We all know that sales positions take up a great deal of time in our lives and most of us are wired this way. I asked her if she was interested in becoming a liaison because it would give her an opportunity to have more flexibility in her schedule and it would increase the financial picture of her family of four. It took about a year or so before she took action to be a liaison. Once she was trained, Stella took off like a firecracker. We watched her grow her market share by 80% in the first quarter. Her numbers have grown year over year ever since. Clearly her perception of her performance as a liaison was not at all accurate. The fact that she decided to act proves that she had some measure of confidence. Sometimes it's the confidence of others that gives us the confidence to take the first step.

You are more than capable. Stella was in her comfort zone as an Admissions Director and she wasn't sure that she would be the same as a liaison. She is now one of the top liaisons in the region.

You're Voice

Your voice has a great deal of power and influence. When you feel stressed or uncomfortable, your voice may tend to shift to a high pitch or your speech may speed up. It's important to be aware of your own situation. Some have strong voices while others have weak ones. A strong voice is less likely to be interrupted and the message is taken more seriously.

A warm voice is received best. Most of our most trusted and inspiring leaders have a warm voice. You can get your voice to sound warmer by bringing your pitch down and smile when you speak. Empathy can also be heard in your voice. I recently admitted a patient and I gave both her and her sister my business card while she was in the hospital. The patient's sister called me about a month later very upset that her sister had just called her with multiple complaints. She was not yelling but her voice was loud and she was noticeably upset. I used my voice to help her calm down on purpose.

The technique of keeping your voice tone low and calm helps keep the other person calm. After addressing her concerns she apologized for her aggression and she said that she actually felt better.

Over Communicate

If you have more than one location. Zero in on where the patient wants to go and where the patient is needed most.

Let's review different handshakes and what they communicate?

Be sure to look the person in the eyes when you shake their hand.

It only takes about 7 seconds for a person to create their opinion of you as you approach. Your hand shake can seal the impression.

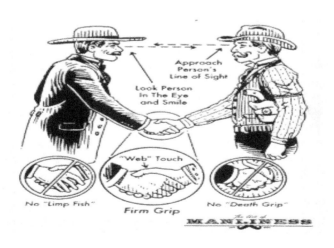

Limp Hand Shake

I don't want to engage you.

TOO Hard!!!

I am going to dominate you.

OR

I was not taught how to shake hands.

Perfect!!

You are happy to meet me and you are confident.

The left hand covers the perfect hand shake. This means that we are in agreement. We are partners.

So let's use this hand shake when you meet.

This says: I am happy to meet you. I am professional.

And this one to end the meeting

This says: "We are in agreement to do business together."

"Listen, or thy tongue will make thee deaf."

NATIVE AMERICAN PROVERBS

Mirroring

This idea is not new, it's just not practiced as much as it could be.

Mimicking VS Mirroring

Parrot's mimic what they hear

Hello   Hello

Repeating the same words, cold and indifferent.

Let's take a look at an everyday conversation to see how mirroring works.

Your customer says: "My cousin heard bad things about your facility. She told me not to go there."

A mimic response: "Your cousin heard bad things about us so, she doesn't want you to come to us."

Mirroring Is:

Repeating the meaning using your own words in a warm and carrying way. Listen carefully. The customer will tell you what to focus on.

Try mirroring.

Your customer says: "My cousin heard bad things about your facility. She told me not to go there."

"**I see** that your cousin's response makes you feel uncomfortable. How long ago did it occur? Would it help if I give him a call to invite him by for a tour and to meet our new staff? **We** could see if there are any questions that I could answer for both him and you?"

Note: The "**I See**" says that you have connected with the customers feelings.

The "**We**" indirectly says that you and the customer are in agreement to come to your facility. Now you just need to get the cousin onboard.

Know What Not to Say

Email, video, texting, social media and voice mail all leave a permanent record. Take this moment to think about it. It's easy to do what everyone else does. But you are not everyone else. You are the Liaison of Choice. This means that you are intentional about how you communicate. You understand that once released, you can't undo it. It could take 3-4 good deeds to erase 1 bad one.

Successful Liaisons don't gossip. If you have an issue with someone, address it with that person. If a person has an issue that doesn't concern you, keep your feelings to yourself. Once you have a reputation of not listening to gossip, people won't bring it to you. Be careful of phrases that start with, "I like Jennifer but……….."

Gossiping is cowardice – saying something behind someone's back that you wouldn't say to their face.

Every Liaison Should Know

Your words can not be unsaid and a person can't unhear them.

Negative gets around faster than positive.

Not everything deserves a response.

Ask Yourself: Does what I'm about to do or say, move me closer to my goals or further away from them? **Remember** that we work in an overlapping community. One day you're working alongside a co-worker and the next day that co-worker is your boss.

Collect names, numbers and emails. Your customers will call you when they need your services. They will let the case manager know that you are their facility of choice. You notice that I didn't say, "Your Company is the facility of choice, right?"

Your customer will follow you because you have built a trusting and caring relationship with them. Companies will want to hire you because you have a Mobil customer base that they can tap into.

This is marketing on purpose 101. It requires time, patience and perseverance.

The Liaison is the only person to communicate with the hospital staff unless the liaison is off or if permission is granted. This cuts down on the miscommunication that can occur when too many people are managing a referral.

Coach Yourself – When you respond to a situation, are you asking yourself, "Am I too emotional right now? How much time do I need to get myself together so I can calm down and respond rationally?"

If you are in a situation that you can excuse yourself, politely do so.

If the situation is constricted, ask, "What would be the most spiritually and emotionally mature response right now?"

When you are taking time off:

Put the dates on your outlook calendar and send invites to everyone that might reach out to you while you're out. Change your voice mail on your phone and let your referral sources know in advance. Be sure that they know how to reach your team. Use your leave. This is a part of maintaining your mental and social wellbeing. This is an area that some sales and marketing people have a problem doing.

Your mental and physical health is imperative to your success.

Take the time to eat right and exercise.

Use your leave from work to reboot. Don't work when you are supposed to be resting or vacationing. Turn off your phone and put your laptop away until it's time to return to work. Tend to your family and yourself.

I've yet to meet a person on their death bed that has said, "I wish I would have worked more."

Remember, it's all about your choices

Have a Mentor or Mentors

Choosing a mentor is a process. No one is perfect and you probably won't find everything that you're looking for in one person. A mentor will have some qualities that you can grow from and others that you simply leave behind.

Find people who have the qualities or skill set that you are striving for and simply ask them to mentor you in these areas. Be coachable and you will grow.

Self-Talk

What self-talk do you practice before interacting with your case mangers on the stressful days? Low census, boss is calling, your numbers are not reflecting your efforts yet?

Have you followed your marketing plan? If yes, the results will materialize soon. If no, why not?

Your marketing results are typically two weeks away.

Speak to your higher/inner power – confirm your belief out loud.

Now that we have covered the basics, let's get to the meat and potatoes of being that Liaison of Choice.

What's Next?

Starting Your Day

Rehabilitation Center/ALF/ Liaisons etc.

Your Day will be dictated by your referrals, customer service rounds and your sales call appointments.

*Answer your electronic systems and emailed referrals first thing in the AM or the night before. Ask for permission to contact the patient or family to offer a tour and to answer any questions. You have 15-30 minutes to answer a referral.

*Check the facility shopping list to see what patients are in your hospital. How many beds are available? Find out the payer and if they are short term or long term so you can inform the case manager on rounds. This will let you know what direction to send your referrals. If there is a concern with a patient returning it needs to be communicated immediately to the case manager.

*Verify that your admissions came in and are applied to the correct account.

Send the Admission Director your "Referral Update report."

Record your admissions from each account in your log.

You are responsible for your accounts both In and out of the electronic referral systems.

*Visit your admissions within 48 hours of admission to assure a smooth transition.

The 1st 72 hours of a patient admitting to your center is usually the most crucial because this is when things tend to go wrong.

* Touch base with the Guardian Angel and the nurse for the patient.

Clinical On-Board Form

Green_____ or Yellow Reason_____

Admit Date_____Patient Name_____Room_____

Gender_____Current Living Arrangement_____

Goals for Recovery STC/LTC   Payer_____

Family Contact_____

Hospital_____Case Manager_____

US Citizen Yes or NO Surgery Yes or No

 Surgery Date_____   Procedure_____

Age_____ DX_____

Allergies_____

Require Hemodialysis in SNF Yes or NO If Yes Provide Checklist

If this is a new dialysis case provide pre dialysis labs

If pt received any dialysis treatments in the hospital within the last 7 days of discharge please send the flow sheets

Past Medical History (PMH)

_____

Height_____ Weight_____ PO Diet_____

J- Tube or G-Tube Yes or No If Yes Type_____

Tube feeding and PO Diet Yes or NO

Immunization:

Date of Flu Vaccine: _____ Pneumonia _____

Wounds/Pressure Ulcers

Send evidence of administration (TAR)

Site(s) Size_____

Wound Infection? NO or Yes _____ C&S Results Attached___

Respiratory   Last 7-14 Days of SNF Admission

Tracheostomy in the Last 14 Days Type_____Size:___Suction frequency: Q_____Hrs

Oxygen in the Last 14 Days

Send evidence of administration

Liter Flow Mask ( ) _____L   Nasal Cannula ( ) _____Non- Re-breather ( ) _____

Vent/Resp in Last 14 Days of SNF Admission   NO or Yes Attach Notes_____

C-PAP Last 7 Days   NO or Yes Settings_____

Bi-PAP Last 7 Days NO or Yes Setting_____/_____

Chest Tube   NO or Yes Type_____

Drains into Bulb_____/Suction_____

IV

IV Therapy in Last 7 days

Send evidence of administration (MAR) be sure that the nurse has signed off on it

Access: Peripheral ( ) PICC ( ) _____cm
Other_____

Antibiotic Ordered? _____Stop
Date_____

Chemotherapy or Radiation Type in Last 14 days No or Yes-
MAR/Note attached_____

Other Clinical

Urinary Catheter Type   Urostomy___Foley____Condom___

Type of Ostomy_____Ostomy Size_____

Isolation Type_____Reason_____

Precautions   Seizure___ Wander Risk___ Locked Unit___
Other_____

Equipment Needs

Specialty Mattress   No or Yes Type_____

Bariatric Equipment   No or Yes Diagnosis of Morbid Obesity? Yes or No

Other Equipment_____

Other

Cognitive   Alert ( ) x_____ Confused ( ) Comatose ( )

Behaviors ( ) _____

Rehabilitation   PT ( )   OT ( ) ST ( )

Goals for Discharge from SNF   PVT Home ( ) ALF ( ) Nursing facility ( )   Homeless ( ) other ( )

_____

Convicted Of a Crime   No or Yes

History of Sexual aggression or Incarceration Yes or No

Notes:

_____

Facility Clinical Capabilities was discussed with patient __

Or representative_____

Liaison Name and Phone Number_____

Support documentation is needed

Last 7-14 Days prior to the discharge date to the SNF

This document assures a smooth transition to the facility and the collection of your data needed.

Patient Driven Payment Method *(PDPM)*

Referrals

Check the insurance first-Don't waste time starting on a referral that you can't accept financially. Know what company does take the insurance that you don't have a contract with, so you can refer the case manager to that company.

* Once you identify how many patients you have not been able to accept because your company didn't have a contract, report the data to see if a contract should be pursued. (Do the same for any equipment and medical diagnosis).

*If you depend on someone else to verify the insurance be sure that you have access as well.

Therapy notes must be within the last 24-48 hours. READ the notes to assure accuracy. This is the most common cause of insurance authorization delays.

Send: On Boarding Sheet, Face Sheet, Chest X-Ray within the last 30 days or a Computed axial tomography (CAT Scan), History and Physical, last 72 hours labs, med list (check for high cost meds), operative reports and dialysis-ventilator checklist.

Physical-Occupational-Speech Therapy notes, the last 72 hours of progress and nursing notes, if Psych – send psych note

Mental Illness and Mental Retardation Screen (MIMR) is **required on every patient** (The hospital fills it out-it addresses the mental illness and mental retardation status-If positive-the patient has to be approved by the state).

Note: Don't ask the case manager to fax or upload something that you have access to. If you don't have access to the hospital computer system you don't have a choice but work on getting that access).

Refer to the PDPM Medicare Requirement Sheet if the patient is Medicare (On page 47).

Check for high cost meds (Check your company policy on patients bringing their meds in from home).

Diagnosis Triggers to watch for (high cost meds)

 Hep C- Med Elbasvir/Grazoperevir or Harvoni (ledipasvir/sofosbuvir) ($1000/pill)

Surgical Patients: Fonda injection

HIV antiviral medications

IV Zyvox 600mg is $71/dose IV $9/pill Liquid $30/day

Cancer Meds are costly-be sure they are priced out

MS-Multiple Sclerosis- over 12 different meds

Transplant Medications are high cost

Narcotics: Send scripts before the patient arrives

Medication Alert: If on Haldol PO see about getting it changed to Haldol Decanoate injection monthly if the patient has a history of not complying with medication administration.

If the patient has an **Old G-Tube** – When did they get it and did they use 100 days of Medicare on that admission? If Yes→The only way you can re-skill this patient is if they are eating 51% by mouth or have stopped using the gastrostomy tube (G-tube) for 60 days.

IV Therapy- If on Intravenous medications the patient may need a line other than a peripheral line. Peripherally Inserted Central Catheter (PICC) need picc line measurement sheet with every PICC. We use this to verify that we have removed the entire line once the medication ends).

Have the IV medication name, dose and the stop date.

Need Settings: vent, wound vac, C-Pap or Bi-Pap get settings. C-Pap is 1 number and Bi-Pap is 2 numbers. If permitted, have the patient bring the C-PAP or BI-PAP from home or the mask from the hospital. The maintenance team can check it out for safety and clear it for use (Check your facility policy).

Tracheostomy's –size, type, age and suction frequency (Suction orders Q shift and PRN) (Know your facility policy on how frequent the suctioning can be)

Wounds-size, location and treatment order Wound Vac – setting is needed___mmHg

O2 – liters and via (route)

Chest tubes by bulb or suction (know your clinical capability)

PDPM as of 10-1-19 for Medicare Patients

(Patient Driven Payment Method)

$ Added to your daily rate

Hospital records required to support the admission of a Medicare patient to a SNF.

If there is not a $ amount noted then the information is needed to add to the MDS point system NTA (Non-Therapy Ancillary).

*Medication Administration Record (MAR) with a signature that indicates that the IV was given

The Last 7 Days prior to discharging to the SNF: $40-$86.21/Day

IV Fluids

IV ABT/IV Push

TPN/PPN/ IV Feedings

IV MEDS

- Treatment Administration Record (TAR) **$28.15/Day**
- Wound treatment-including stage 3 & 4
- 2 or more Stage 2's

- Open Lesions
- Surgical Wounds

Major Organ or lung transplant- Current or History

Infected wounds need culture and sensitivity result **Informational Not $$**

Morbid Obesity (If there is a diagnosis of obesity, please clarify if the diagnosis is obesity or morbid obesity).

Morbid Obesity **adds to the NTA (Non-Therapy Ancillary Rate on the Minimum Data Set (MDS)**

Malnutrition

C-PAP/BIPAP **$19/Day**

Last 14 Days: Prior to Discharging to the SNF

Oxygen **$14/Day**

Suctioning/Chemotherapy/Radiation **Informational No $$**

Tracheostomy **$140.66/Day**

Ventilator/Respirator **$384/Day**

Transfusion **$78/Day**

Hemo or Peritoneal Dialysis (Even 1 Day) **$28.15/Day**

Isolation **$78/Day**

C-Diff or Respiratory (Patient can't leave the room services have to come to them)

Case Studies

Case Study #1

74 yo female, Medicare patient with the diagnosis of MVA (motor vehicle accident), fracture right hip, pneumonia and dehydration. She was in ICU for 2 days. The patient has been admitted for 6 days and is ready to discharge to a SNF.

What do you need to admit?

Standard admission paperwork previously listed.

Use your critical thinking skills: The motor vehicle insurance name, phone number, policy number and the claim number for the accident. The hospital staff doesn't usually capture this information. You should obtain it in your bedside interview. If it was a "Hit and run", notify your facility and proceed with the medical insurance.

Notes that indicate that the following was done:

The Last 7 Days prior to discharging to the SNF: Add an additional daily $ for the referral when you send MAR's – IV fluids and hydration $40 - $86.21/Day

Last 14 Days: Prior to Discharging to the SNF Oxygen $14/Day

Treatment Administration Record (TAR) **$28.15/Day**

C-PAP/BIPAP **$19/Day**

Case Study #2

24 yo female Medicare patient admitted with ESRD, COPD, morbid obesity, anemia. She was brought to the hospital via 911 and was admitted into ICU with acute respiratory failure and COPD exacerbation.

Other than the standard paperwork, what do you need?

Notes that indicate that the following was done: Within the **last 14 days** of discharge to the SNF

- Oxygen $14/Day
- Transfusion **$78/Day**
- Hemo or Peritoneal Dialysis (Even 1 Day) **$28.15/Day**
- Ventilator/Respirator **$384/Day**

Last 7 Days

- C-PAP/BIPAP **$19/Day**
- IV fluids/ABT$40-$86.21/Day

COMMUNITY AND INTERNAL MARKETING

Community Marketing

Your community marketing starts with everything within a 25 mile radius of your facility and of the top 3 Zip Codes of the patients that are admitted to your hospital accounts. This is on your ahd.com report. Goggle hospitals, nursing centers, hospice centers and companies that provide hospice care, car and bike clubs, churches, dialysis centers, vascular centers, libraries, social clubs, elementary schools (host an art show) health fairs, HIV and methadone clinics.

Internal marketing

Your staff needs to know that they count. The simplest things go a long way. A bag of candy to pass out to the staff that is taking care of your patients. Whenever someone brings particular staff members to your attention because of awesome service, reward them with lunch.

Remember that all of you are each other's customers.

MAKING ROUNDS

Hospital Rounds and Greeting the Case Manager

Hospital integration – get to know the hospital hierarchy team (Vertical Integration) (Refer to your AHD data for the number of employees in the hospital).

- Who are the Key players?
- Who is the leader on each floor- Official and Unofficial.
- C-Suite
- Case Management Department
- PT/OT/ST/RT
- Receptionist, unit clerks, nurses, maintenance, house keepers, transporters, security, garage staff, techs etc.

Who are the other Liaisons in your Hospital and how can you partner with them?

- SNF's
- Home Health
- Hospice
- IV Infusion, Pharmacy
- Ins Companies
- ALF

Put your cell phone on vibrate.

Absolutely NO GUM chewing.

Smile and Speak to everyone

Each site has their own culture – you'll find that out when you make rounds.

When rounding – be a resource but stay out of the way.

Pay attention to the nonverbal Language.

Key Account Management

*Give examples of body language that tells you that's its ok to come in and sit down?

The staff might:

Turn their chair around towards you.

Stop what they are doing and sit still.

Pull up a chair for you.

Body Language that tells you to leave:

The staff might-

Make a phone call.

Turn their chair towards the desk.

Start shuffling papers.

What does it say about a liaison that calls the case manager every day without being asked to do so?

You're desperate for patients and not willing to make rounds.

Don't leave more than 5 brochures and a card

What is the message when you leave 10 or more brochures with the Case Manager?

You're not coming back any time soon.

"Do my work for me."

What is best practice when providing lunch or gifts for customers?

Have everyone sign an in-service sheet.

Provide lunch not to exceed $10/person while providing an educational experience.

Note: Sometime you may need to do an impromptu in-service. Have them sign the in-service sheet and send the follow-up lunch to them at their convenience. Ask them what they prefer to eat. Don't assume what they might want to eat.

Some facilities are not permitted to accept, cups, pens or pads and others are. When your customers can accept gifts, they should have your company logo on it.

When and how should you take the temperature of your effectiveness in your accounts?

Ask the case manager how you're doing.

Analyze your market share.

When you walk into the room, what are people saying about you?

(You only get one reputation)

How do people feel when they are around you?

When you make rounds, the case manager keeps telling you "All of my patients are going home." How can you verify this information discreetly?

Observe whether there are discharge packets addressed to other SNF's on the case manager's desk or in the chart rack.

Touch base with the other SNF's liaisons to see how there referrals are going.

If you suspect that the statement is false, what is your next step?

Give the case manager a report on how well the last patient that they gave you is doing.

Let the case manager know that the referrals have decreased and that you want to be sure that you are providing optimum service. Ask for honest feedback.

Service Recovery

Mr. G told the case manager that he doesn't want to return to your center. You meet with him and he gives you his list of concerns:

1. The staff NEVER answer the call light.
2. The nurse tried to give him someone else's medication.
3. He doesn't have a TV in his room
4. Some staff members are rude.
5. He also lets you know that 3 staff members are great.

What is your approach?

Always take notes while you are speaking to the patient. Apologize to the customer. Assure the customer that you will follow them into the facility if they chose to give you another chance to get it right. Let him know that you will be reporting his experience to the facility leaders and you will let the 3 employees that did a great job know that they made a difference. "I will be treating them to lunch." Report the concerns back to the facility right away. Reach out to his Guardian Angel (facility based program that has department heads assigned to check on each room daily) as well.

If the patient decides to return, exchange phone numbers and be sure that you follow through.

Be sure to let the case manager know that you are addressing his concerns and you are rewarding the three employees that he complimented.

Check on your hospitalized patients

Give your business card and a stuffed bear or gift. Verify that they plan to return.

Be aware of any customer service issues and if there is a reason that the patient can't return let the case manager know immediately.

Bedside Sale:

See every patient without exception and be sure to drop in on them daily until they admit to you. If they have any changes in the plan to come to you, you will pick up on it before it's too late.

Always Knock on the door and **wait** until you are invited in. (Use hand sanitizer before entering the room and wash your hands before you leave).

Introduce yourself and shake hands. Give them your business card.

"Hello Ms. Johnson, I am Glenda with Hopkins Care Services." (If others are in the room ask the patient if it is ok to speak in front of them) (If the patient has dementia be sure to treat them with the same respect).

Shake hands

Give out your brochure and business card.

"I am working with your case manager Jenny to help you get approved for skilled rehabilitation. Has your doctor spoken with you about going to a rehabilitation center once you leave the hospital?"

"You have been accepted into Bayside Rehab. I stopped by to introduce myself and to see if there were any questions that I could answer for you and to be sure you know what to expect. Have you ever been in a rehab center before?" Ask if there any issues with pain. If the answer is yes, ask if what they are on is working and tell the patient to be sure that they take pain meds prior to discharging from the hospital. The ambulance ride to the facility may cause them additional discomfort. If the patient is on a narcotic, be sure you send the script over prior to the patient coming.

Explain how the insurance and rehab works.

Exchange cell numbers (you have a direct line to your customer while in your care and after they discharge home).

Role Play:

Demonstrate how you would explain how Medicare/MCO/MA works.

Medicare: It is helpful to explain the insurance verbally and nonverbally. Many people are not aware of how their insurance works. Use your hands while speaking. This helps people remember what you said.

Medicare gives you 100 days to stabilize in the rehab center.

Days 1-20 are covered at 100%.

Days 21-100 Medicare has a $170.50/day co-pay.

If they have a co-insurance, explain how many co-pay days it covers. If the patient or family member doesn't react to the co-pay amount they may not have understood what you said. Confirm that they understand.

MCO (Managed Care Organization)

Explain that your insurance case manager will report their progress weekly to the insurance company. Once the patient has reached his goals, he will be discharged.

If while in rehab there are any pain issues or if the patient doesn't feel well, they should report it immediately. The insurance company wants to see continued progress. It is important that the patient participates in therapy, if not they will be cut and discharged to home earlier than expected.

Cover – Facility location

How therapy works: Therapy works with you___ days/week and _____ times/day. Physical Therapy will work with everything from the waist down: walking, balance and steps.

Ask: How many steps to your front door?

Once in the home, can you live on that level or are there more steps?

Do you live alone?

Occupational Therapy will work with you on everything from the waist up: dressing, bathing, if you need any adaptive equipment for reaching.

(If there are any pain issues—be sure that the patient is comfortable with what the hospital has them on (Knee surgery patients experience a lot of pain) be sure that the patient takes pain medication before leaving the hospital if they are experiencing any pain at all, the ride to your facility could be bumpy).

Tours- Ask the patient if there is anyone that you should be speaking to other than them to answer questions or to invite them by for a tour of your facility.

If you have enough leeway, ask?

Would you prefer a bed by the window or the door? (Asking for the business)This helps to secure the sale.

"Is there anything that I can have in your room when you arrive that would make you comfortable?"

Examples: newspaper, snacks, plant, flowers, clothes, etc.

What makes you Unique as a Liaison?

How do you know when you are the preferred provider?

Referral sources tell others to refer to you.

They add you to the patient choice list that is given to the patient.

They call you for advice on cases.

They refer to you regularly.

Handling Objections Role Play

Patient: "I heard horrible things about your facility"

You: What did you hear? How long ago was that?

Always Confirm that it is true and let them know what has been done to correct the issue.

You: "Yes Fareway Heights did have issues in 2013, but they have since provided customer service in-services to the entire staff and new hires. The management team rounds more frequently and I will be there to follow-up with you as well within 24 to 48 hours of your admission. "You are not alone. "I will be checking on you on my rounds at the facility and you have my cell number if you need to speak to me before I arrive."

Extend an invitation for a friend or family member to tour.

?? Can you go right in to see the patient once you get the referral?

Once you know your hospitals, you will know if it is ok to make contact with the patient immediately.

Ask the Case Manager how to proceed once they send the referral. Some are ok with you contacting the patient but **others are not**.

You can only speak to someone other than the patient if the patient gives you permission. After speaking to the patient you should ask. "Is there anyone that you might want me to speak to so I can answer any questions about rehab?"

Sitters/Wanders Need 24 hours without a sitter if it is not for falls for some facilities (Know your policy).

Be careful to interview this patient. If the patient has a sitter because of combative behavior, hospitals may need to use drugs to keep them calm. If the patient is always sleeping when you go by to see them wait until they are alert so you can assess their behavior. Check the medications that the patient is being given and the last time they received it.

If the patient has a sitter because of wandering behavior, assess as to whether he/she is easily redirected. If yes, a wander guard system may work. If No, the patient should be assessed for a locked unit.

Being comfortable with feeling uncomfortable allows you to push pass your fears:

Sometimes you need to ask the tough questions:

What were you incarcerated for?

Why didn't you send your mother back to the hospital when you saw that she wouldn't let you care for her?

INSURANCE COVERAGE

Insurance

Medicare A Pays for the room/board and therapy.

Medicare gives you 100 days to stabilize.

Rehab Center – Days 1-20 are covered 100%, Days 21-100 Medicare has a $170.50/day co-pay.

In most cases the patient must be admitted for 3 midnights to qualify for Medicare. There are some areas that do not have to meet the 3 midnight rule.

Once used, the Medicare days reset after the patient is away from all skilled services for 60 days.

Military hospitals don't use Medicare but if the patient is hospitalized in these hospitals, it is still considered a skill service.

Medicare B covers dialysis and equipment/outpatient therapy/ facility doctor.

Non skilled stay patients – therapy is billed, enteral, ostomy /wound care.

Medicare D covers medications.

Tricare covers the SNF and all of the co-pay days (depends on the policy).

Commercial Insurance

May cover some of the co-pays but it depends on what the patient purchased.

Each insurance has its own contract. Get a copy your facilities Insurance Cheat Sheet so you can make informed decisions about your referral. It should tell you the reimbursement for medication, equipment, treatment supplies etc.

Before requesting an authorization:

Get the insurance company contact and phone numbers.

Be sure to have therapy notes no older than 48 hours of the discharge date. Read the notes before sending. (This is the #1 cause of holding up the authorization).

Have the intravenous type, medication name, stop date and equipment needs.

Your insurance case manager or designee will work with the insurance company to get the authorization to admit. Once admitted to the SNF they report week to week on the patient's progress until the patient is stable and ready to discharge.

Medicaid – medication cost is not a concern - Medicaid has a formulary – if the meds are not on the formulary, the alternative will be ordered or prior authorization paperwork will be submitted by your facility. State coverages may vary.

PVT Pay- Get your room and board cost.

MAKING YOUR MARK

Answering in the electronic system

Each hospital is different so you need to know your case managers.

Check the system and answer within 15 minutes. If you are waiting for someone to verify the insurance be sure to accept the patient medically. "Medically accepted checking ins now."

Always thank them for the referral.

Document in the system daily.

What are the 4 types of case managers?

Know their cases very well.

Don't really know their cases.

Like for you to assist in the entire process.

Some would rather you simply stay in your lane.

<u>HIPA Compliance Required</u>

Phone and computer- internet security (use initials when texting).

Use a shredder in your home office.

What is the only thing Constant in Life?
Change!

Be open to change. Don't let it stress you out.

Play Nice in the Sand Box

You will be working in the same accounts with your competitors.

You may not be able to take a patient.

You may not have what the patient is requesting.

There will be cases that both of you are accepting. Be sure that you handle this professionally. **Remember**: One day you're working side by side and the next day that same liaison could be your supervisor.

What makes you different from your competitor?

Why would a Case Manager want to direct referrals in your direction VS your competitor?

How often should you give a report on how a case managers' patient is doing in your care?

If you are new to the referral source, let them know within 24 hours of the admission with a follow-up in 2 weeks.

Customer Service

Your Customer Service will make or break you.

Follow-up within 48 hours to check on the patient once admitted. Do you have an internal program that checks on your customer once they are admitted?

Visit your hospitalized patients and bring them a gift. A plant or stuffed bear with the company logo, or it might say get well soon.

Don't forget that your organizations staff are your internal customers.

(What are you doing for them?).

Dress appropriately and never chew gum.

Mistakes are easier to forgive when the customer likes you!!

Riding Out your Highs and Lows in Census without feeling Stressed

Don't wait for your supervisor to bring low numbers to your attention.

Show that you know what you are doing especially if the numbers are down: Holidays are tough on Rehabilitation Centers because patients want to be at home. Your strongest marketing strategies need to be 3 weeks prior to any holiday.

1. Know your market share: What numbers came from the account prior to you and in the prior years. Know why your numbers have shifted. Never wait for your manager to bring a concern to you. You articulating this information is your first line of defense.

2. Follow through with your account strategies that you developed from your analytic reports.

3. Do at least 4 sales calls a week with your pre call planning sheets filled out.

Pre-Call Plan

Client Name Title:

_____

Meeting Location and Date/Time:

_____

Brochures/Material you will use:

_____

Initial Benefit Statement "The purpose of the meeting
is…."_____

Referral History:

_____

General Back-
ground_____

What topics will the meeting agenda cover? Key features in the brochure:

_____

Open-ended questions to ask…

"What are you looking for in a rehab center partner?"_____

Anticipated Clients/Referral Concerns

Objections/Resistance:

_____

Your Response:

_____

Your Companies "Benefit VS Competitor"

Closing: What closing question will you ask?

_____

Follow-Up

Strategies_____

ASK FOR THE

BUSINESS!!!!!!!!!!!!!!!!!!!!!!!!!!!!!!!!!!!!

A Liaison doesn't just go out and ask for the business, they create opportunities for the company and become a referral source for the customer.
 *When your team sees this data, you are given more time to complete your goals.

Don't expect that all of your strategies will work. 60% of them will show you what doesn't work.

What are the differences between Hunters and Gatherers?

Hunters: search for the right patients, get a commitment to admit and follow the patient every day until they are stable to admit.

Gathers: get a lot of referrals but most of them don't admit.

What is the most important trait of an amazing Liaison? **TRUST**

Your Choices will Make or Break you as a Liaison

List 5 Things that will **Make** a Liaison?

Being trustworthy (always telling the truth)

Reliable

Follows through

Always in contact

Easy to find

List 5 Things that will **Break** a Liaison?

Not honest, gossips

Hard to contact

Doesn't return calls

Doesn't follow through

Accepts a patient, then says that the patient can't come

 How do you handle your stress?

 Who are you venting to?

Use caution when choosing this person. You tend to say things to them that you would not want repeated.

Ask – "How Can You Make It Happen?"

Share an example of when everyone else said "NO" but you found a way to make it happen?

<u>Maintain Accurate Records:</u>

How Many: Denials and Why

What is the next step? When you find that you are denying certain diagnosis or insurances repeatedly, see if your company should be looking at it as an opportunity to grow.

What is your A/I Ratio- Admit to Inquiry Ratio?

Divide your admissions by your inquires

20 Admits / 30 Inquiries = 0.667 or 67%

Stay off the Radar

You supervisor is dealing with a great deal. Your job is to be sure that you stay in compliance, be supportive and do your best at all times. Don't be that employee that make your boss's job stressful.

Data Collection

Liaison Account Statistics

Account Name_____

Month/Year_____

#MC_____ MCO_____ MA_____ PVT PAY_____

Of referrals_____

Of Admits_____/# Of referrals_____ =

Conversion Ratio%_____

Pending_____

Bedside Sales_____

#Bedside Sales Admits_____

Bedside Sales not Admitted_____

Reasons for not admitting_____

MC admits from home_____

Market Share Worksheet

Account_____

Number of total Medicare dis-
charges_____ ÷ 12 = _____x .07_____ =
The Approximate Medicare dis-
charges/month to a SNF

Now

Add 20% to account for the other payers

_____

This gives you the approximate number
of discharges to SNF's
Monthly_____

How many referrals/month do you re-
ceive? _____

What is the %_____?

What is your conversion ratio? _____%

Notes:

_____

Keep track of your Admits and Referrals

_____Hospital Admits Month_____Year_____

Date	Room	Name	Payer	Case Manager	Facility	Notes

Don't forget to track the daily rate of your admissions. This information will become most valuable if you ever have to prove your wealth to your company.

_____Hospital Referrals Month_____Year_____

Date	Name	Payer	Case Manager	Facility	Bedside Sale

Your Real power

Is In

Seeking

Common

Ground

Being Liked

We can agree that you won't be liked by everyone, but the objective is to keep in mind that people always remember how you make them feel.

Be your best self. Seek to be kind, authentic and helpful. This won't look the same every day. You're going to have good days and bad days, you're human. But even on your worst days, there is still a better version of you in that state. It's not your best but it's better than your worst.

Your ability to influence people is linked to whether or not they like you. This is not suggesting that you rearrange who you are to make people like you, but you want to be aware of the impact of your actions and behaviors on others. Make changes that feel authentic.

Back in my 20's I was the charge nurse of a 60 bed dementia unit. Our unit frequently won contest that the facility had on many different subject matters. One year we won the unit of the month because we prevented skin breakdown on our patients. Our team was strong and we worked hard to be the best. I always received high scores on my evaluations and I was a rising star within the organization. One year, we had a new supervisor start with the company. When she gave me my evaluation she said that I needed to smile more. "Smile more? What did that have to do with anything?" I was sure that she was going too far. I was very upset about her comment. This bothered me all day. When I got off work I called my mother.

My mother wasn't just my mom, she was my mentor and my hero.

This is how that conversation went:

Me: "Mom, I had my evaluation today and my new supervisor told me that she loved how the unit was caring for our patients but that she wanted to see me smile more."

"I don't have to smile if I didn't want to."

Mom: "Are you finished dummy?" My mother would call me a dummy with endearment. It was her way to get my attention not to be hurtful.

Me: "Yes, ma'am."

Mom: "Is it going to take anything away from you to smile more? Is your choice not to smile more going to move you closer to your goals or further away from them?"

I had to take a breath and consider that she might be right.

Me: "O.K. I will try it to see what happens."

This shift didn't exactly feel authentic to me but I did it because Mom made it sound like the right thing to do. It ended up changing how my supervisor viewed me. My next evaluation was even higher and she wrote in the comment section that my smile made the difference. Go figure, it worked!

When it comes to you influencing others, you actually have a great deal of control over it. Simply smiling more made my supervisor increase my evaluation score.

Finding common ground is the key to influencing people. Look for things that you have in common with other people instead of how different you are. Develop a habit of noticing common experiences, interests or backgrounds with people.

Now, I took a marketing class in the 90's with an instructor that told us to survey the area once we entered into a customer's space. We were to look for pictures, awards, statues or even a room deodorizer to connect with. She wanted us to find something in that room that we may have in common so we could bring it up in conversation. I interpreted the message as being manipulative and insincere. I couldn't have been more wrong. It took me some years to understand what the instructor meant. She simply wanted us to see what we had in common so we could build on it. If I had gotten it back then, I would be further ahead today.

The lesson to learn here is that you purchased this book on purpose. Take the information without prejudice and use it to accelerate your liaison carrier to the next level. **Become The Liaison Of Choice** on purpose.

SOOOOOO!!!!!!

How far did you get on your list of 200 things that you want?

You have to be prepared to go through a few things to get them.

Some complacent people around you will be uncomfortable when they see you striving towards your goals.

They will:

Be jealous

Gossip about you

Be crabs in a barrel

Lie on you

Discourage you

Put you down

Discount what you're doing

Block your efforts

Look for you to fail

So look at it this way, you must be succeeding because if you weren't, they wouldn't have anything to talk about.

Stay motivated and we will see you at the top.

Don't take any time to address the naysayers. Keep climbing the ladder. If you stop to address them, you slow down your climb.

It's all about your choices

Ask
For The
Business

Ask for What You Want

Salary

You first need to know what you know. Woman have a tendency not to ask for what they are worth vs men. Are you pricing yourself too low or too high?

If you are a new liaison, your salary will probably be at the lower end of the salary range and your renegotiation power will be on your evaluation date. But, the fact that you have taken the initiative to purchase this book in an effort to craft your skills ahead of time tells me that you should negotiate in the middle salary range. This number is outside of any bonus structure present. Bonuses can and probably will change every year. Consider bonuses as the sprinkles on the cake after the cake and frosting are prepared. You can't budget your life expenses on bonuses.

Once you start working for a company, it's likely that your increases will not be substantial in a year. This number could be 0-7% so negotiate strong in the beginning. Now, don't miss out on the fact that money is not your only motivation for compensation. Vacation time, working from home, company car, company credit card and mileage reimbursement all play a role in your decision. Write out the pros and cons on a piece of paper prior to this discussion so you are prepared to close the deal at that meeting. When you finalize the meeting, seal it with your handshake that says, "We are in agreement." Cover the shake with your left hand. If you are new to this position and you have taken extra steps to prepare for it such as taking classes, following the road map of this book, obtained mentors to assist you, you should feel empowered to request a higher salary. So, that might look like this. Once you get to the salary negotiation part of the interview, accept the lower end with an increase in 6 months once you improve the previous market share numbers by 25% or more. Yes, this is a bold move on your part. Or is it?

Consider a few of things:

1. The company knows that you have not performed in this capacity before, but they are interviewing you because they are interested in you.

2. You are demonstrating to them that you are not afraid to ask for the business whether it's for yourself or for the company as a whole.

3. Be sure to get the agreement in writing with no exception. Never rely on a person's memory or the fact that they will still be employed with the company in 6 months.

4. Some women tend to agree to lower salaries and don't ask for raises. Men are four times more likely than women to initiate negotiations. No wonder the salary gaps are so far apart. So when it comes to income, women start at lower salaries and then continue to avoid negotiation throughout their carriers. Woman stand to lose more than $500,000 by the age of 60. Push through the fear

of asking and do it anyway. The answer is no if you don't ask. If you're already a great negotiator whether male or female, this is a reminder. But if you are like most people, who never ask for what they want, this is for you.

Once you have asked for what you want take a breath and stop talking. Sometimes we stack questions on top of each other when we are uncomfortable with a subject matter and are concerned about the response we might get. Resist this urge. Once a bold question is asked it may take the other person a moment to gather their response.

Give the person time to respond. Always ask for the business at the end of your sales call. Some sales people do all the work to get the meeting, prepare for it, handle themselves on the sales call accordingly and then don't ask for the business. This is not you. The Liaison of Choice always asks for the business.

"NO" is Not a Dirty Word

The Word "NO"

Doesn't mean "NO!"

It means not right now

Chose to take the fear out of the word.

So, you've written out your business plan and you're ready to execute your 25 sales calls for the month. Chances are, you will hear the word "NO" before you get to the end of your list. Some sales people create a game of it. "Let's see how many NO's I can get before I get to the end of my list." Now hearing the word "No" is a win not a loss. The other approach is what we discussed earlier. "No" simply means, not right now.

Understand What You Want

Understand what you want. Then open up your mouth and ask for it.

Be ok with not always getting what you ask for. That "No" provides clarity and direction. It could lead to a conversation towards a modified "Yes". Once you ask for what you want, don't allow nervous energy to cause you to apologize for asking or to undo your original request. I was recently at a repass. One of the family members that was in her early sixties shared that she was in a relation with a lovely man who treated her fine but she wanted someone who had more things in common with her. She described her ultimate sole mate. "I want someone who is adventurists, likes to go out and try new things. I want a man that wants to travel." OK, she knows what she wants. Then she proceeded to say she should probably just be happy with what she had.

Don't let nervous energy cause you to apologize for asking or to undo what you want.

This goes back to your choices.

When you underestimate your value, you may expect less from others and therefore ask for less.

Note: People use cues that you give to quickly determine key information about you so use this to your advantage. Be intentional about your communication. Watch the responses to verify that what you intended to communicate actually made it through.

I am a new grandmother of two. I had my son at a young age so the lessons that I have learned over the years puts me at an advantage for my adult son and my grandsons. I was recently at a going away party at work for one of our directors when I got into a "Light Bulb" conversation with a co-worker who is expecting her first grandchild. We both expressed the purposeful efforts in communicating with our adult children and how we were going to facilitate the growth of our grandchildren. Our efforts have already become purposeful, productive and positive. We are building generational wealth and an environment for them to thrive in **on purpose**. Now this is not to say that most grandparents don't do this. It's simply stressing the point that we are both operating on purpose to create something that our parents could not. We chose not to operate as a leaf being blown by the wind. There is no difference with your being that "Liaison of Choice." This must be a purposeful creation. It will not happen by accident or by chance. You have to make it happen. The most successful liaisons are not fearless they're simply courageous.

Public Speaking

Public speaking is uncomfortable for some people. Here are some tips that will help you push through that feeling. Put yourself in situations on purpose to practice this skill. The only person that knows you're doing this is you. You will become more comfortable with each encounter. You won't be able to be as successful as you should if you don't speak in public comfortably.

I was at an event that had 3 representatives at their table. Their tenure with the company ranged from 2 months to 7 years. The organizer told them that they would be given time on the microphone to introduce their company to the audience. All 3 of them had a look of panic on their faces. The employee who had only 2 months with the company said that she would speak. When I saw their level of discomfort, I shared with them a few tricks to ease the pain. I suggested that they walk around and have conversations with people or stand in front of their table to greet people as they walked in the event doors so they wouldn't be speaking to strangers once they stood in front of the room. When you engage the audience prior to speaking to them, they share things with you in conversation that may be useful when you speak.

It's all about your choices

The only one that decided to take the advice was the employee that was new to the company. The other two stayed behind the table where they were comfortable. Companies are looking for Liaisons that can help move their business to the next level so please, feel the fear BUT do it anyway.

Not being prepared can make you uncomfortable, so plan ahead.

Pack your event supplies early

Don't wait to pack your supplies the day of the event. Pack them 2 nights before or have your supplies prepacked and labeled. Make a checklist and verify that everything is present. Pack: Table cloth, business cards, brochures, candy jar, candy (don't forget the sugar free option), giveaways, a clip board with your contact form to capture your future customers information, a large giveaway or game of some sort to engage the customer. Your notes in bullet point formation and any props that you might be using.

Arrive at the event early

Give yourself plenty of time to get to your event. Allow for unexpected traffic delays or a flat tire. Once you have set up, walk around the area to get the feel of your environment and engage with the others. Put your chair behind your table and stand in front of the table.

Pause
Pray
Proceed

PAUSE-PRAY-PROCEED through a Pandemic

First of all, this is not all about money and keeping your job during a pandemic.

The 2020 COVID-19 Pandemic brought the world to its knees. Companies suffered tremendous financial losses and staff loss their jobs.

What does the **Liaison of Choice** do in this situation?

1. Be a **Team Player** like you have never been before while maintaining your quota.
   A. There will be an opportunity to assist in picking up PPE supplies and deliver them to facilities.
   B. If you are a nurse, you can work shifts in a building.
   C. You can support the Case Management staff by covering insurance verifications.
   D. Partner with Community Organizations to help your activities departments provide social distancing activities to help keep the patients spirits up. COVID-19 created an

unwanted social distancing environment that made it difficult for many of us. Our activities staff arranged a mobile parade of family members and local car clubs with signs to display their Love outside their cars. It was an amazing site to see the families and friends go through followed by a parade of Corvettes.

2. Reach out to restaurants to send food to the Facility Staff.

3. Volunteer in the facility to answer call lights on your days off.

4. This is a time to get admissions from sources other than your typical locations. If you are a hospital Liaison, approach Nursing Homes, Assisted Living Facilities, community organizations of all types. COVID-19 is a threat to everyone. If organizations know that your organization is prepared to care for patients with any diagnosis, they will feel confident about

coming to you for their care when it's needed.

5. Be that "Breath of Fresh Air" for your supervisor. Offer solutions, not problems. Support your leader in every way that you can. Think outside the box and leave the lid open for your great ideas to come out.

6. With COVID-19, nursing facilities are segmented in 3 zones - Red, Yellow and Green Units. Be sure to speak to the patient and any other person that is involved in making the decision to go to a rehabilitation center.
Be prepared to explain how your company is protecting the staff and their patients. Prospective patients and family members want to feel confident about choosing you. Many will chose to go home without going to rehab because they are fearful of going to a Nursing Facility where they are more likely to contract the virus. If a Medicare patient goes home, they

have 30 days to change their minds and decide to come to a rehabilitation center without returning to the hospital.

Be sure to continue everything that you were taught throughout this book.

- Answer the referral source within 15 minutes.
- Make contact with the patients and or support person.
- Over document in your computerized systems so that any and everyone understands where you are in the referral process.
- Don't allow a pandemic environment cause you to handle the stress inappropriately. Do what you need to do to keep your stress level down and continue to give 100% and more.
- Keep your A/I Ratio at least 70% (Admission to Inquiry Ratio) we don't need Gathers - We need **Hunters**!!!!!!
- Take advantage of opportunities like being a COVID tracer. The government is looking for COVID trackers. They provide free training on line and you can

earn money from home if you get laid off. Search your health Department website for this information.

- You could start your own business making masks in your home or through an online partner.

Now, all of that being said. I'm not saying that you won't be laid off during this challenging time when you do everything that we just covered. You will be the last on the list because you have proven your value.

I am promising that when your company is forced to make staff cuts, you will have done all that you could do to support the companies objectives and you will have built an amazing resume. You will know that you have done everything that you could do. Continue to hold your head up high.

Put your Higher Power First

Your Family is next and Your Money will follow.

In the words of one of my most admired Supervisors - Valerie Beatty.

"PAUSE-PRAY-PROCEED"

Last But Not Least

There are 3 types of Liaisons:

The one that watches things happen.

The one that makes things happen.

And the One that says,

"What the heck just happened?"

Which one are you?

Made in the USA
Monee, IL
07 March 2022